Finding Colors

Yellow

Moira Anderson

Heinemann Library
Chicago, Illinois

© 2006 Heinemann Library
a division of Reed Elsevier Inc.
Chicago, Illinois

Customer Service 888-454-2279
Visit our website at www.heinemannlibrary.com

Editorial: Moira Anderson, Carmel Heron
Page layout: Marta White, Heinemann Library Australia
Photo research: Jes Senbergs, Wendy Duncan
Production: Tracey Jarrett
Printed and bound in China by South China Printing Company Ltd.

09 08 07 06
10 9 8 7 6 5 4 3 2 1

Library of Congress Cataloging-in-Publication Data
Anderson, Moira (Moira Wilshin)
  Yellow / Moira Anderson.
      p. cm. -- (Finding colors)
  Includes bibliographical references and index.
  ISBN 1-4034-7447-8 (lib. bdg. : alk. paper) -- ISBN 1-4034-7452-4 (pbk. : alk. paper)
  1. Number concept--Juvenile literature. I. Title: Numbers. II. Title.
  QC495.5.A539 2005
  535.6--dc22   8672

                                                    2005009727

Acknowledgments
The author and publisher are grateful to the following for permission to reproduce copyright
material: APL/Corbis/Richard Cummins: p. **18**; Rob Cruse Photography: pp. **5** (boots) **9, 11,
23** (boots); Corbis: pp. **13, 21**; Getty Images/Brand X Pictures: pp. **14, 23** (petals); Getty
Images/Digital Vision: p. **16**; Getty Images/PhotoDisc: pp. **20, 22, 23** (beach); PhotoDisc:
pp. **4, 5** (banana, helmet, toy duck), **6, 7, 8, 10, 12, 15, 19, 23** (banana, toy duck, helmet),
24; photolibrary.com/Goodshot: pp. **17, 23** (hay).

Front cover photograph permission of Tudor Photography, back cover photographs permission
of PhotoDisc (toy duck) and Rob Cruse Photography (boots).

Many thanks to the teachers, library media specialists, reading instructors, and educational
consultants who have helped develop the Read and Learn/Lee y aprende brand.

Contents

Some words are shown in bold, **like this**.
You can find them in the glossary on page 23.

What Is Yellow?

Yellow is a color.

What different colors can you see in this picture?

The color yellow is all around.

Have you seen these yellow things?

What Foods Are Yellow?

Bananas are yellow.

You peel the yellow **skin** to eat the banana inside.

Some cheese is yellow.

It is made from milk.

What Yellow Clothes Can I Wear?

This raincoat is yellow.

A raincoat will keep you dry in the rain.

These yellow boots are made
of **rubber**.

They keep feet dry in the rain.

What Is Yellow at Home?

This toy duck is yellow.

It is made of **plastic**.

This towel is yellow.

After a bath, it is good for getting you dry.

What Is Yellow on the Road?

This sign on the road is yellow.

It shows that a fire station is near by.

This yellow garbage truck is
on the road.

It takes away the garbage.

What Is Yellow in the Park?

There are yellow flowers in the park.

They have lots of yellow **petals**.

There is a yellow slide in the park.

The park is a good place to play.

What Yellow Things Are on a Farm?

There are yellow chicks on a farm.

Chicks are baby chickens.

Some animals are fed yellow **hay**
on a farm.

What Yellow Things Are at the Beach?

This umbrella is yellow.

It protects people from the sun.

People can wear yellow flippers at the beach.

Flippers help people to swim.

How Do People Use Yellow at Work?

People can use yellow trucks to move dirt around.

Some people wear yellow
helmets at work.

Helmets help keep people safe.

Quiz

What yellow things can you see?

Look for the answers on page 24.

Glossary

hay
dried grass for feeding animals

helmet
strong covering worn to protect
the head

petal
colored outer part of a flower

plastic
a strong, light material that can be
made into different shapes

rubber
a strong, stretchy material used for
making things like boots and shoes

skin
outer layer of a fruit or vegetable

Index

Answers to the quiz on page 22

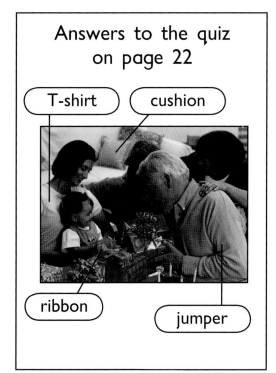

T-shirt   cushion

ribbon

jumper

Notes to parents and teachers

Reading non-fiction texts for information is an important part of a child's literacy development. Readers can be encouraged to ask simple questions and then use the text to find the answers. Each chapter in this book begins with a question. Read the questions together. Look at the pictures. Talk about what the answer might be. Then read the text to find out if your predictions were correct. To develop readers' enquiry skills, encourage them to think of other questions they might ask about the topic. Discuss where you could find the answers. Assist children in using the contents page, picture glossary and index to practise research skills and new vocabulary.

DEC   2010